Cell Group Leader Training

Leadership Foundations for Groups that Work

Participant's Guide

M. SCOTT BOREN and DON TILLMAN

CGR
CellGroup
RESOURCES

Cell Group Resources™, a division of TOUCH® Outreach Ministries
Houston, Texas, U.S.A.

Published by Cell Group Resources™
P.O. Box 7847
Houston, Texas, 77270, U.S.A.
800-735-5865 • Fax (713) 742-5998

Cover design by Don Bleyl
Text design by Rick Chandler
Editing by Blake Egli

Library of Congress Cataloging-in-Publication Data

Boren, M. Scott.
    Cell group leader training : leadership foundations for
groups that work : participant's manual / M. Scott Boren and
Don Tillman.
    p. cm.
    Includes bibliographical references.
    ISBN 1-880828-39-1
    1. Church group work. 2. Christian leadership. 3. Small
      groups—Religious aspects—Christianity. I. Tillman,
      Don. II. Title.
    BV652.2 B67 2002
    253'.7—dc21
                                            2001007702
                                                CIP

Cell Group Resources™ is a book publishing division
of TOUCH® Publications & Outreach Ministries, a resource
and consulting ministry for churches with a vision for cell-based
local church structure.

Find us on the World Wide Web at
http://www.cellgrouppeople.com

Contents

Introduction

Peter told the leaders of the church, "Be shepherds of God's flock that is under your care, serving as overseers — not because you must, but because you are willing, as God wants you to be; not greedy for money, but eager to serve; not lording it over those entrusted to you, but being examples to the flock" (1 Peter 5:2-3).

I (Scott) grew up on a farm with a small flock of sheep. My feelings toward them were less than amicable. They were loud, always making an awful "baaaaaaing" noise to get more food. They stunk (imagine four inches of dense wool after a rainy winter), and had to be shorn every year to get that hot, smelly wool off or they could die in the heat. They always had their lambs on the coldest days of the year and early in the morning, requiring special attention. And they had to be penned in every night because sheep are so vulnerable that wild animals will attack them if they are left in the pasture.

Think about how many times God refers to us — the most intelligent beings in creation — as His sheep. If anyone but God were to call us that, we would be offended.

In Matthew 9:36, it says, "When [Jesus] saw the crowds, he had compassion on them, because they were harassed and helpless, like sheep without a shepherd. Then he said to his disciples, 'The harvest is plentiful but the workers are few. Ask the Lord of the harvest, therefore, to send out workers into his harvest field.'" During His time on earth, Jesus could not minister to everyone by Himself. So He enlisted workers to help Him minister to the scattered sheep. Today He is calling people like you and me to gather scattered sheep and care for them in cell groups.

Introduction

While on the farm, I did not have the heart of a shepherd, but I saw someone who did, my father. Whereas I threw rocks at the sheep to scare them into the pin, my father had only to open the gate, and they came running. I would wait to tend to them until it was convenient for me; my father would consistently care and watch over them no matter what the cost to himself. I barely knew the differences between the sheep, but my father remembered the last lamb of each sheep; he knew when each was expected to lamb next and how to best care for each one.

I (Don) have never raised sheep, but I have shepherded God's people and have, in turn, been shepherded by others. It does not amaze me that God would liken you and I to sheep: we are sheep! We need God's care and supervision as well as that of a shepherd leader.

The idea of caring for sheep leads me to think of the people you will lead. Yes there will be messy times, but there will be even more times of joy as others are transformed because of your ministry. What greater blessing can there be than to walk with Jesus, caring for His sheep?

You may be thinking that this calling is a high one, one beyond your abilities. If so, you are in a very good place spiritually. This job is not for those who are so confident in their abilities that they do not depend upon the Lord to do the work through them. You are called to intimacy with your Chief Shepherd who cares for you. As He shepherds you, you will be able to shepherd others.

Peter tells us, "And when the Chief Shepherd appears, you will receive the crown of glory that will never fade away" (1 Peter 5:4). Get ready to embark upon the greatest adventure of your life, one with eternal rewards.

Dean Miyema & Jodi
Randy Hoak &
Sandy Lincoln & Judi
Lenny Trapp & Janelle
Tony Mucich & Beth
aline Sat. the 25th

SESSION

Gregg's Sue
Mark & Holly

1

- Open hearts for
existing Bible
Study Leaders.
Ministry Lead
Person
- Point Person
Keep this going

Preparing Your Heart
for Cell Group
Leadership

"You know that I have not hesitated to preach anything that would be helpful to you but have taught you publicly and from house to house." — Acts 20:20

Preparing Your Heart for Cell Group Leadership

Multiple Kinds of Small Groups

PERSONAL ACTIVITY

Check the various kinds of groups that you have experienced.

- ☐ Task Groups
- ☑ Mission Groups
- ☑ Choir Groups
- ☑ Bible Study Groups
- ☑ Worship Groups
- ☑ Fellowship Groups
- ☑ Discipleship Groups
- ☑ Care Groups
- ☑ Recovery Groups
- ☑ Evangelism Groups
- ☑ Leadership Development Groups
- ☑ Intercessory Prayer Groups
- ☑ Sports Groups
- ☑ Sunday School Groups
- ☑ Altar Ministry Groups

[handwritten: Cohesive approach / Support/Coaching Training on going]

[handwritten: Martin Luther, John Wesley, Small groups]

Effective Cell Groups are Holistic

[handwritten: Involve & touch people in every facet of their lives]

- A group of 4-15 people.

[handwritten: N+N-N (2-15)]

- Members gather <u>weekly</u> for scheduled meetings.

- Members <u>support one another</u> through unscheduled, life-giving interaction. *[handwritten: love, prayer, calls, emails]*

- Members reach out to the hurting world. *[handwritten: group focus]*

[handwritten: reaching out - pray for relatives, co-workers, neighbors, friends]

- New leaders are mentored and released. *[handwritten: develops & expands God's kingdom. replication]*

- Group multiplication is a goal.

[handwritten: Ch. plant - Community care groups]

> "No Christian can grow strong and stand the pressures of this life unless he is surrounded by a small group of people who minister to him and build him up in the faith."[1] — Chuck Colson

Biblical Foundation for Holistic Cell Groups

- Great Commandment
  - Upward — Love God
  - Inward — Love People

[handwritten: Love God w all heart, soul, mind & strength, & neighbor as self]

- Great Commission
  - Outward — Preach the Gospel
  - Forward — Make Disciples

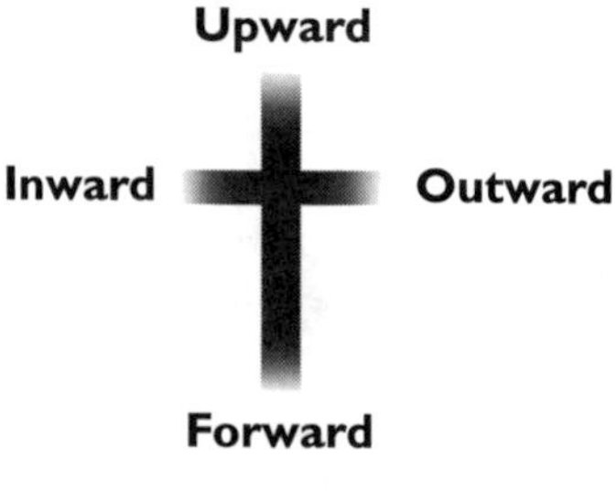

[handwritten: All authority has been given... Therefore go & make disciples, baptizing them in the]

Upward

Inward **Outward**

Forward

Why the Great Commandment and the Great Commission?

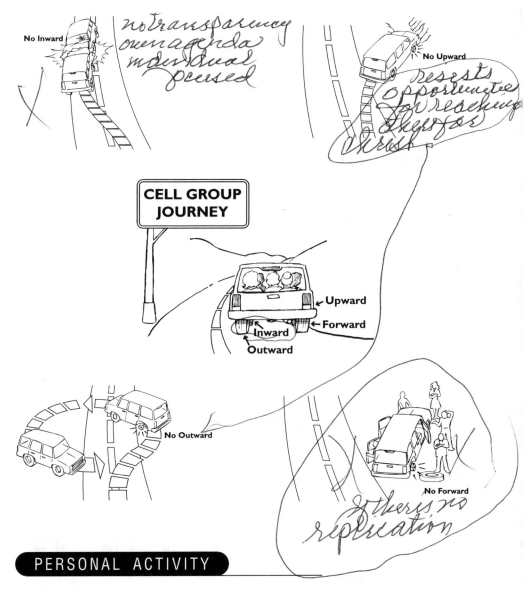

No Inward

no transparency
own agenda
manual
paused

No Upward

resists
opportunities
for reaching
others for
Christ

CELL GROUP JOURNEY

Upward
Forward
Inward
Outward

No Outward

No Forward

there is no
replication

PERSONAL ACTIVITY

Circle the component that was the strongest in your last (or current) small group experience. Place an "X" on the weakest.

The Heart of an Effective Leader

• The call of the heart!

- Not a job

• Heart of a shepherd (John 10:11-15)

Jesus Contrasts

SHEPHERD	HIRED HAND
Cares to point of sacrifice *LAY DOWN HIS LIFE*	Quits when it gets tough
Knows sheep personally *Intimacy INDIVIDUAL RELATIONSHIPS*	Knows sheep as a flock
Intimate relationship to God	In it for personal advancement
Heart for the sheep	Just doing the job

• Shepherds are **not**:

    - Super-Christians

    - Bible teachers

    - Pastors

    - Super Saints

Sheep need the shepherd.

They have a heart for people.

The Characteristics of Shepherds

A leader is defined by the group that follows them.

• A shepherd has a flock.

• A shepherd leads.

    - They do not drive

• A shepherds gets close to the sheep.

making day to day contact with the sheep

> "How do you get sheep smell on you when you don't touch them —
> except for a handshake and some quick words in the aisle Sunday
> morning?"[2] — Lynn Anderson

• Cell group leadership is about getting close to people.

So you can speak into their lives requires some time outside the weekly mtg & church to get to know the sheep intimately.

SMALL GROUP ACTIVITY

We were invited by Tony to be involved —

Share why you have chosen to attend this training.

Even though we've been involved in sml. group ministry it's good to have an opp. for ongoing training & getting on the same page.

What do you hope to learn through this training?

Everything I need to know to be an effective co-leader

affinity & inviting need people leaders but group participants too.

Preparing Your Heart for the Great Commandment

> "Love the Lord your God with all your heart and with all your soul
> and with all your mind. This is the first and greatest commandment.
> And the second is like it: Love your neighbor as yourself."
> — Matthew 22:37-39

Upward — Love God

I must have a

- Passion for (intimacy) with God *that stimulates*

    - Cell group ministry (flows out of love for God.)

    - Groups don't work well when leaders lead out of:
        Performance ✓
        Guilt ✓
        Compulsion ✓

    - Your regular time with the Lord dictates whether you will minister out of your own abilities (the flesh) or out of the fullness of God (the Spirit).

- How to prepare your Upward life: *don't worry about* *Focus on the Lord, the lesson, the surroundings etc.*
    - Spend the last 30 minutes to an hour before the cell meeting praying, worshipping, and interceding for group members.

    - Fast.

    - Pray over the location of the meeting <u>before</u> people arrive.

I can only go as deep w/ people as I've gone deeply č God.

Inward — Love One Another

God
- Love for people

    - People need love to enter into transformation.

need to feel unconditional love & acceptance.

Leaders play a key role in providing an atmosphere conducive to this.

- God extends His love to create a safe place for those who don't know love.

- When you pray for your cell members, God will reveal how to love them.

> "Thus this spiritual love will speak to Christ about a brother more than to a brother about Christ. It knows that the most direct way to others is always through prayer to Christ and that love of others is wholly dependent upon the truth in Christ."[3] — Dietrich Bonhoeffer

• How to prepare your Inward life:

   - Pray daily for your group members.

   - Let God transform your heart for them.

   - Listen to God's Word for them.

   - Share what you hear God saying.

Warm welcome - hugs, smiles.
positive outlook.
Pray faithfully, follow up on prayer requests
listening
helping c practical needs
Calls, e-mails, cards, flowers
Set the tone - enthusiastic
loving, sensitive & caring
talk is cheap, but involvement
& sacrificial love is costly, but required.

15

Preparing Your Heart for the Great Commission

all authority has been given to Me,

> "Therefore go and make disciples of all nations, baptizing them in the name of the Father and of the Son and of the Holy Spirit, and teaching them to obey everything I have commanded you. And surely I am with you always, to the very end of the age." — Matthew 28:19-20

Outward — Penetrate the Lost World

- Cell groups depend upon a "go" strategy. *good news*

  Take the love of God & His influence

  - They do not rely on "come and see" methods.

  - They take the message to hurting people.

- Group leaders lead people to "go" through:
  - Service
  - Missions
  - Sacrifice
  - An open-door policy
  - Building relationships with unbelievers
  - Inviting new people
  - An "Empty Chair"

- How to prepare your Outward life:

  - Ask God for compassion for the lost.

  - Pray for the lost. *Annette & Brgan, Jordon, Dylan*

  - Befriend a lost person.
  no agenda

16

Forward — Mobilize Disciples

- **Forward** takes place through:

  - Discipling new believers – *Baby Christians — Showing others how to live for Christ —*
  - Mentoring new leaders – *train leadership Share*
  - Launching new groups – *Invite & recruit people to join, train new leaders, start a new group — Talk early about these, pray so it is the plan —*

- The future of your cell group ministry depends upon the development of future leaders.

  - Without them, forming new groups is impossible.

  - Without them, current leaders must do all of the ministry.

  - Without them, current leaders often burn out.

- How to prepare your Forward life:

  Offer opportunities

  - <u>Delegate</u> the practical tasks of the meeting.
    <u>Snacks and drinks</u>
    <u>Phone calls</u>
    host home

  - Pray that God will <u>raise up new leaders.</u>

> "Ask the Lord of the harvest, therefore, to send out workers into his harvest field." — Matthew 9:38

SMALL GROUP ACTIVITY

Where did you mark the "X" on page 11?

Why do you think your group struggled with that component?

What can you do differently to change your next group?

Recommended Reading

• *How to Lead a Great Cell Group Meeting* by Joel Comiskey, Introduction, Chapter 1.

• *Leading From the Heart: A Group Leader's Guide to a Passionate Ministry* by Michael Mack.

Cell Leader Call Description

The word of the Lord came to me: "Son of man, prophesy against the shepherds of Israel; prophesy and say to them: 'This is what the Sovereign Lord says: Woe to the shepherds of Israel who only take care of themselves! Should not shepherds take care of the flock? You eat the curds, clothe yourselves with the wool and slaughter the choice animals, but you do not take care of the flock. You have not strengthened the weak or healed the sick or bound up the injured. You have not brought back the strays or searched for the lost. You have ruled them harshly and brutally. So they were scattered because there was no shepherd, and when they were scattered they became food for all the wild animals. My sheep wandered over all the mountains and on every high hill. They were scattered over the whole earth, and no one searched or looked for them.'" — Ezekiel 34:1-6

Since God reprimands the shepherd for not doing these things, the call of the shepherd cell leader is:

1. To strengthen the weak.

2. To heal the sick.

3. To bind up the injured.

4. To bring back the strays and to seek the lost.

5. To lead gently and not harshly.

SESSION

2

Getting a Meeting
Off the Ground

Let us hold unswervingly to the hope we profess, for He who promised is faithful. — Hebrews 10:23

Getting a Meeting Off the Ground

SMALL GROUP ACTIVITY

Describe in a minute or less the most memorable party you have ever attended.

What happens in a typical cell meeting?

SEGMENT	FOCUS	FLOW
WELCOME (20 MINUTES)	**Icebreaking**	You to Me
WORSHIP (20 MINUTES)	**Jesus**	Us to God
WORD (40 MINUTES)	**Discussion and Ministry**	God to Us
WITNESS (10 MINUTES)	**The Lost**	God through Us

Welcome - Helping People to Connect

- The benefits of icebreakers:

    - They prepare people to share openly.

    - They help people connect with one another.

    - They warm up the atmosphere and ease tension, especially when the cell members don't know one another well.

- Basic Instructions:

    - Make it natural.
      Don't say, "The icebreaker for tonight is . . ."
      Instead, just ask the question as if it were part of conversation.

    - Answer the question in a circle.
      This facilitates participation by all group members.

    - Whoever asks the question answers it first.
      This sets a pattern for others to follow.

- Find an icebreaker that will work for your group.

    - For new groups, choose a light-hearted, "get-to-know-you" question.

    - For established groups, ask questions that go deeper.

- When someone new is visiting, help him or her feel comfortable. A question that causes laughter is often good.

- If children are present, include them.

- Don't overwhelm the members with a threatening question.

• Delegate the leading of the icebreaker to a cell member.

- See *303 Icebreakers*, published by Cell Group Resources™ for more ideas and a detailed guide for leading a great icebreaker.

• Potential icebreakers include:

- Who was your hero when you were a child?

- When you were a teenager, who was your best friend? Do you still stay in touch? Why or why not?

- What is your favorite movie? Why?

SMALL GROUP ACTIVITY

Choose one of the three icebreakers above and share your answers with one another.

a learned skill, requires prayerful preparation—

Worship - Experiencing the Presence of Jesus

- Focus the group on Jesus.
  - Not worship songs
  - Not a group lesson
  - Not even people's needs

"When Jesus becomes the agenda, all other agendas are realized."[1]
— Bill Beckham

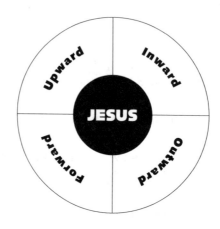

- Jesus at the center of the group is the key.

"For where two or three come together in my name, there am I with them." — Matthew 18:20

26

• Ask yourself these *Key* questions:

- What does Jesus want me to do in the group?

- How is the Holy Spirit ministering to people tonight?

- Where is God leading the group?

ask God to rekindle my First Love - those signs that have left Him

Guidelines in Leading Worship

• Be a worshipper.

- Worshippers carry with them the fragrance of Christ.

- The group will go as far into worship as you lead them.

> *"A worship leader is someone who heartily loves God, gives expression to that love and effectively leads others in expressing their love for God."*[2] — Gerrit Gustufson

• Pray, Plan, and Practice.

- Ask God for a focus or a theme.

- Select songs to suit the theme.

- Rehearse all the songs you have chosen.

- Plan how to link the different songs.

- Plan a time for sharing an appropriate Scripture or releasing words of encouragement.

• During the Worship:

- Lead by being observant and sensitive.

- Be in charge of the session. Even if you are unsure or nervous, do not tell people.

- Although you have prepared a certain format, always allow the Spirit to lead you.

- Expect God to be present.

• Things to avoid when leading Worship:

- Avoid an impromptu selection of songs. Prepare beforehand.

- Avoid long introductions and comments between songs.

- Avoid choosing songs that the cell members do not know.

- Avoid linking songs in different keys.

- Don't insist on singing all the songs that you have prepared.

• Creative ways to Worship in a small group

- Share short testimonies about the good things God is doing or has done.

- Share answers to previous prayers.

- Read a short section of scripture and meditate on God's word for a few moments.

- Sing a capella songs of praise and worship.

- Use a worship CD with well-known choruses to lead the group.

- Use the Psalms for group worship.
    Read a section of the Psalms.
    Share your favorite Psalm.

- Sentence prayers offered by everyone in the group

- Alphabetic praise where people contribute attributes of God alphabetically, i.e. A-Awesome, B-Big, C-Compassionate, etc.

Structures Provide Guidance

- Remember: Stay flexible

  - The 4 W's are not a fixed structure.

  - If you are prepared spiritually as a leader, you will want to flow with the direction of the Lord.

- Watch out for ruts and routines.

- Meet in His name, not in the name of structure.

This session focused on the first two parts of a meeting, Welcome and Worship. The Word portion will be addressed in Sessions 3 and 4 — and the Works in Session 6.

Recommended Reading

- *How to Lead a Great Cell Group Meeting* by Joel Comiskey, Chapter 2.

- *303 Icebreakers*, Introduction.

3

How to Facilitate Ministry in the Cell Meeting

Instead, speaking the truth in love, we will in all things grow up into Him who is the Head, that is, Christ. From Him the whole body, joined and held together by every supporting ligament, grows and builds itself up in love, as each part does its work. — Ephesians 4:15-16

to minute middle segment

How to Facilitate Ministry in the Cell Meeting

Facilitate, Facilitate, Facilitate!

• Facilitation provides the <u>legs</u> that the group walks on.

   - The goal is to facilitate ministry in the group, not to have the leader "do" the ministry.

   - When you facilitate, allow God <u>to work through the group.</u>

   - When cell leaders are facilitating well, they often speak only *20* – <u>30%</u> of the time.   *40 min - a group*

• Facilitate *application*, not *information* during the Word portion of the meeting.

   - Most people "know" more Bible information than they practice. *We're educated for beyond our obedience*

   ✗ - The cell is the place where people <u>apply</u> the Word to their lives.

   - If a discussion does not lead to the implementation of truth, then it has failed.

BEWARE OF PREACHING AND TEACHING

- Most people have experienced the "knowledge-based" group.
  - Each question has only one correct answer.

- In these groups, only those with the knowledge can share.
  - This communicates that God only uses certain people.

- The leader "knows" more and therefore tells people what to think.
  - Dismisses the valid and valuable thoughts of group members.

- The cell meeting is not the place for the solo preacher or teacher.
  - It is the body of Christ working together, building up each other.

Ask Open-Ended Questions

- Limit the use of closed questions that elicit short, specific answers.
    Examples: Based on John 3:16,
      - Who was Jesus addressing?
      - Who are the Pharisees?
      - Does God's love extend to the Pharisees and Nicodemus?

- Open questions provide an opportunity for interaction.
    Examples:
      - How have you experienced the love of God?
      - What does it mean to you that God gave His life so that you can have eternal life?

• Types of Open-Ended Questions

- Observation Questions ask what the passage says.
  Examples:
  - What is the command given in Jesus' Great Commission?

- Interpretation Questions inquire about the meaning and provide an opportunity for group members to understand the passage.
  Example:
  - What does it mean to make disciples?

- Application Questions bring the discussion to the real issue: "How does this apply to me?"
  Examples:
  - Who did God use to reach you?
  - How has God used you in the past to reach people for Him?
  - How can we as a group participate in the Great Commission?

Cautions: judgment necessary - discern where the group is - w/ Pre-Christians he specifically open to house anyone new.

GENERIC QUESTIONS THAT YOU CAN USE WITH ANY SCRIPTURE PASSAGE:

1. What stands out to you in this passage?

2. What seems to be the main point of this passage?

3. Can you illustrate this truth from an experience in your life?

4. What is God saying to you right now?

LARGE GROUP ACTIVITY

Write Observation, Interpretation, and Application questions for the following passage:

Do nothing out of selfish ambition or vain conceit, but in humility consider others better than yourselves. Each of you should look not only to your own interests, but also to the interests of others.
— Philippians 2:3-4

Observations Questions:

1.

2.

Interpretation Questions:

1.

2.

Application Questions:

1.

2.

3.

Listen

- Seek first to understand, then to be understood.

    - Ask others what they think before you share.

    ✗ - Don't plan what you are going to say while others are talking.

    (- Affirm people when they share.) *Thank them,*

    - Restate what you hear the person saying.

> *"To 'listen' another's soul into a condition of disclosure and discovery may be almost the greatest service that any human being ever performs for another."*[1] — Douglas Steeve

- Show interest with your posture.
    - *smile*
    - Lean forward.

    - Don't cross your arms.

    - Nod your head.

- Listen to what is not said.

    - 60% of communication happens through body language.

    - Watch for: *- tone of voice*
        Disinterested stares
        People sitting outside the circle
        Tears
        Short answers
        perfunctory responses

- Refuse to answer your own questions.

  Don't fill it up c̄ your words

  - Even if silence follows.

  - Restate the question for clarity.

  - Sometimes people need to think about their answer for a few minutes.

- Invite further responses.
  - *Someone who hasn't shared add something here!*
  - Some people need an invitation to share.

  - Address a question to a specific person if he or she has not shared much.

LARGE GROUP ACTIVITY

Make a list of various actions that communicate that a person is not listening.

Lead the Word Portion into Edification

- Edification is <u>not</u>:

  - Spiritual problem solving.

  - Sharing similar past experiences.

  - Asking questions about a person's past traumas.

  - Identifying people's flaws.

- Edification is:

  - Building up and affirming a person in truth.

  - Speaking the truth in love even when it requires confrontation. *Preferably in private or when the group is comfortable together*

  - Spurring one another to love and good deeds.

  - Letting the Lord minister through other people in the group. *Ask the members of the group to ask the Lord to fill them*

  - Praying for one another. *& with.* *E His Spirit & Truth.*

> "What shall we say, brothers? When you come together, everyone has a hymn, or a word of instruction, a revelation, a tongue or an interpretation. All of these must be done <u>for the strengthening of the church.</u>" — I Corinthians 14:26

- A work of God, not of man.

  We can only speak truth into people's lives as the Lord directs. *They can only hear as He opens the eyes of their understanding.*

- Leading people to the cross so that Christ can do the real ministry.

• An Edification Process

- Identification

  Listen to the Lord to discover the roots of the problem.

  People often share the fruits of the problem, not the underlying root source.

- Confession

  Lead people to acknowledge the underlying issue that has been covered up.

  Without confession, it is difficult to minister to the real need. *of sin Christ's blood was shed for sin.*

- Speaking forgiveness

  Affirm that the person is forgiven and loved of God.

- Edification

  Speak the truth to build up the person.

SMALL GROUP ACTIVITY

- Case Study 1

    For three weeks in a row, Jim arrives late because of work. When he shares in the group, he complains about work and how it is dragging him down. How would you respond?

- Case Study 2

    Sharon shares that her husband is a very difficult person. He does not spend any time with her. He spends every Saturday watching football and working on his '66 Mustang. She spends five minutes bashing her husband. What do you do?

- Case Study 3

    Since she started coming four weeks ago, Jennifer has not talked very much in the cell group. Tonight she breaks out crying saying that since she left home a year ago she has gotten involved in a homosexual lifestyle and that her girlfriend left her. She knows it is wrong, but she loves Holly even though she feels abused by her. How do you minister to Jennifer?

- Case Study 4

    Jerry has been a member of your church for 40 years. He loved to teach Sunday school, but he wants more friends and started coming to your men's cell group. For three weeks now, he has distracted the group from ministry and talked about the original meaning of Paul's teaching in the passage you are discussing. How do you handle this situation?

- Case Study 5

  Bill shares in a mixed gender cell group that his thought life has not been "above reproach." In fact, he had been visiting some filthy web sites over the last couple months. Carrie, his wife, breaks out in tears and storms into the bathroom. What do you do?

- Case Study 6

  Michael is a new Christian. He arrives at the group and announces that he broke up with his girlfriend of six years this week. You can see that he is glad he did it, but that he is a little scared at the same time. How should you minister to him?

- Case Study 7

  Terry just lost his job. You know about it and you know how depressed he is. When someone asks how he is doing, he says that he is fine and that God is blessing him. How do you handle this situation?

Recommended Reading

- *How to Lead a Great Cell Group Meeting* by Joel Comiskey, Chapters 3, 5, and 6.

SESSION

4

Practicing Transparent Communication in a Meeting

Now the Lord is the Spirit, and where the Spirit of the Lord is, there is freedom. And we, who with unveiled faces all reflect the Lord's glory, are being transformed into His likeness with ever-increasing glory, which comes from the Lord, who is the Spirit.
— 2 Corinthians 3:17-18

Practicing Transparent Communication in a Meeting

Five Levels of Communication[1]

1. Surface Communication

    - Public information which most people feel safe sharing.

    - Includes external events like the weather and the news.

2. Factual Communication

    - Information concerning observable ideas and facts.

    - Discussion at this level is safe (e.g. what the scripture passage states, not what it means in someone's life).

3. Thought-Provoking Communication

    - People take some risks at this level as they share their opinions about a topic.

    - Some stop at this level and hide behind debates over ideas.

4. Emotive Communication

  - At this level, people take the risk of sharing how they feel.

  - This requires a deeper level of trust.

5. Transparent Communication

  - Highest level of risk

  - At this level, people share their deepest fears, dreams, and thoughts

"When we are committed to building a safe environment where people can ask stupid questions and be encouraged, reveal their sins and be forgiven, and share their deepest fears and still find acceptance, then we are on the way to building authentic Christian community."
—Thom Corrigan

INDIVIDUAL ACTIVITY

Think about the last small group meeting that you attended. What level of communication did it achieve?

- ☐ Surface Communication
- ☐ Factual Communication
- ☐ Thought-Provoking Communication
- ☑ Emotive Communication
- ☐ Transparent Communication

SMALL GROUP ACTIVITY

Write examples of _____ Communication.

Transparency: The First Door

- Transparency happens when people take off their masks and let others see who they are.

- Transparency requires honesty.

- It is very difficult for a cell group meeting to continue over the long term, if group members are not willing to become transparent.

Vulnerability: The Second Door

- Transparency leads to vulnerability.

  - When you become vulnerable, you let others speak into your life and influence your thinking.

"... Sometimes the only way we can see our talents objectively is through the eyes of others ..." — Unknown

- Vulnerability requires trust.

  - Transparency + Trust = Willingness to become vulnerable.

- Questions of trust:

    Do I trust you to handle what you see in me?

    Do I trust God to speak truth through you that can change my life for the good?

LARGE GROUP ACTIVITY

Make a list of hindrances to transparent communication in a group.

Transparent Communication as a Cell Group Leader

• Model openness and trust.

- Leaders lead.

- If the leader is not willing to be transparent, the group members will not trust enough to open up to the group.

- Don't fall into the perfection trap.

  - Leadership does not require perfection.

  - Cell leaders don't have all the answers.

    The cell leader is not the Savior.

- Be honest when you need prayer.

  - Choose to be vulnerable and let others encourage you.

- Ask for help from group members.

  - Delegate tasks that are not your strengths.

- Deal with hidden sin in your life.

  - Confess major struggles to your pastor.

- Don't hesitate to receive affirmation.

  - Many leaders are ashamed of their God-given strengths.

  - God did not bless his people so that they could belittle themselves.

Creating an Environment for Transparent Communication

- Give permission for group members to reveal their struggles.

- Affirm those who share their struggles.

- Lead the group to commit to confidentiality.

- Don't give or allow others to give "pat" answers to problems.

    - "Everybody struggles with that."

    - "Just pray about it."

    - "Well, the Bible says . . ."

Lead the Group to Transformation

    Transparency
+ Vulnerability
+ Edification
    _____
    Transformation

"Therefore confess your sins to each other and pray for each other so that you may be healed." — James 5:16

Confessing sin is like jewels - they need to be handled w/value, care, delicately, sensitively

PERSONAL ACTIVITY

On a scale of 1 to 10, 10 being high, how easy do you find it
to share transparently with others in a small group?

Uncomfortable   Shares Freely

0   2   4   6   8   10

SMALL GROUP ACTIVITY

Why did you rate the question above at the level you did?

What do you want to see done differently in your next cell group
to promote transparent communication?

Mare

What is one attribute you possess that will contribute to making you an effective group leader?

- As each person responds, the others in the group should affirm what they see.

Recommended Reading:

• *How to Lead a Great Cell Group Meeting* by Joel Comiskey, Chapters 4 and 7.

5

Life Outside the Cell Group Meeting

But the fruit of the Spirit is love, joy, peace, patience, kindness, goodness, faithfulness, gentleness and self-control. Against such things there is no law. — Galatians 5:22-23

Life Outside the Cell Group Meeting

AWANA KIDS

LENNY TRAPP
503.846.1114   trappistview@comcast.net

When you see the word "Family" what images or words come to your mind?

The Two Parts of a Cell Group

The Part	The Meeting	Outside the Meeting
Time	1.5-2 hours	6 days and 22 hours
Place	Home	Everywhere
Method	Discussion agenda	Personal interaction
Requirement	Attendance	Love

More than a Meeting

- Many groups have great meetings, but the life stops when the meeting is over. *Hebrews 10:25 -*

- The Family of God provides a solid metaphor for Body Life.

  - Families are families all the time.

  - In healthy families, people do not choose whether or not to relate to one another.

  - Family members "rub shoulders."
      They get on one another's nerves.
      They forgive one another.
      They sacrifice for one another.
      They help one another.

"The best ministry generally doesn't occur during a group's meetings so much as between the meetings. Every chance you have to touch people between meetings helps them become excited enough to want to come to the next meeting."[1] — Carl George

- We do not have time in a weekly meeting to be the family of God.

  - The only choice is to be family for one another during the rest of the week.

What do you think happens to a group that only has a weekly meeting and no outside interaction?

The Purpose of the Meeting in Body Life

• It is a catalyst for Body Life.

• It provides a time for sharing about life outside the meeting.

• It connects people who are unconnected in Body Life.

• It provides a place to celebrate what God is doing in the group.

• The meeting is not:

  - The place for all of the ministry.

  - The time when all needs are met.

Key Elements of Body Life

- <u>Edify</u> one another:

  "Therefore encourage one another and build each other up, just as in fact you are doing." — I Thessalonians 5:11

  10-12

- <u>Love</u> one another:

  "A new command I give you: Love one another. As I have loved you, so you must love one another." — John 13:34 - *36*

  "Now that you have purified yourselves by obeying the truth so that you have sincere love for your brothers, love one another deeply from the heart." — I Peter 1:22

- <u>Forgive</u> one another:

  "Be kind and compassionate to one another, forgiving each other, just as in Christ God forgave you." — Ephesians 4:32

  31-32

  "Bear with each other and forgive whatever grievances you may have against one another. Forgive as the Lord forgave you." — Colossians 3:13

I Cor 12:24-25 equal concern for one another.

- <u>Pray</u> for one another:

  "Therefore confess your sins to each other and pray for each other so that you may be healed. The prayer of a righteous man is powerful and effective." — James 5:16

  (15-17)

Ps 145:7-9
Keep my

healing
restoration
is the goal

emphasis; one another living in community

• Serve one another:

> "You, my brothers, were called to be free. But do not use your freedom to indulge the sinful nature; rather, serve one another in love." — Galatians 5:13

• Offer hospitality to one another:

> "Offer hospitality to one another without grumbling."
> — 1 Peter 4:9

• Teach and admonish one another:

> "Let the word of Christ dwell in you richly as you teach and admonish one another with all wisdom, and as you sing psalms, hymns and spiritual songs with gratitude in your hearts to God."
> — Colossians 3:16 (15-17)

How do I respond in times when I am angry or frustrated c someone.

LARGE GROUP ACTIVITY

Make a list of the things that hinder groups from participating in Body Life.

Be quick to hear, slow to speak, slow to anger —

Slave to sin vs. a slave to righteousness

Pastoral Care in the Body

- Normally we expect the "pastor" to do all of the pastoral care:

  - Visiting people in the hospital.

  - Praying for the sick.

  - Calling those who have been out.

  - Following up on visitors.

  - Counseling and praying for hurting people.

  - Leading people to the Lord.

- As a cell group leader you are an <u>under-pastor.</u>

  - Cell group leaders work under the authority of the pastoral leadership of the church.

  - Share with your pastor how you are ministering to your group members.

  - If you don't know how to give pastoral care, ask your pastor to show you how.

reschedule my priorities to make time for CLF's
Pray faithfully for those in authority.
Home Prayer Visit

• The next step after doing it yourself: facilitating pastoral care between cell members.

- Pray that they will care for each other.

- Show people how to care for one another.

- Take cell members with you on prayer visits.

- Encourage them to call and care for each other.

Your Ministry Outside the Meeting

1. Dream - Dream of leading a healthy, growing, multiplying group.

2. Pray - Pray for group members daily.

3. Invite - Invite new people to visit the group weekly.

4. Contact - Contact group members regularly.

5. Prepare - Prepare for the group meeting.

6. Mentor - Mentor apprentice leaders.

7. Fellowship - Plan group fellowship activities.

8. Grow - Be committed to personal growth.

- The tool *8 Habits of Effective Small Group Leaders* will help you make these a regular part of your life.

- It is often good to work through this tool with your cell coach.

"Those who have never been a part of a warm family unit, who have lived lives of self-sufficiency for many years and who have been betrayed in trust relationships, will need special encouragement."[2]
— Ralph W. Neighbour, Jr.

Practical Ways to Facilitate Body Life

- Use the phone.
- Invite someone over for dinner.
- Baby-sit for a couple so they can go out.
- Help someone move.
- Tackle a mission project together.
- Establish a prayer chain.
- Sit together at weekly worship.
- Have a half-night of prayer.
- Hold a group fast.
- Set up mentors and/or accountability partners.
- Have a "guys night out" or a "girls night out."
- Make home prayer visits.

SMALL GROUP ACTIVITY

As you look at taking the next step in ministering to others through a cell group, what do you feel like God is saying that you should do differently to be more effective?

HOME PRAYER VISITS – *VISIT THE MEMBERS*

• Choose a night to visit members' homes.

• Arrange a time when you will come to a cell member's home.

• Arrive with a prayerful attitude.

• Ask:
  - How are you doing?
  - Do you have any specific needs we can pray for?
  - Do you have any friends or family members who need the Lord that we can pray for?

• Focus your prayers on blessing the members and their homes.

• Share a relevant scripture.

• Stay no longer than 30 minutes.

Recommended Reading

- *8 Habits of Effective Small Group Leaders: Transforming Your Ministry Outside the Cell Meeting* by Dave Earley.

- *Upward, Inward, Outward, Forward: Improving the 4 Dynamics of Your Cell Group* by Jim Egli.

PRAYER CHAIN

Name: _____

Phones: (H) _____ (W) _____

Name: _____

Phones: (H) _____ (W) _____

Name: _____

Phones: (H) _____ (W) _____

Name: _____

Phones: (H) _____ (W) _____

Name: _____

Phones: (H) _____ (W) _____

Name: _____

Phones: (H) _____ (W) _____

Name: _____

Phones: (H) _____ (W) _____

Name: _____

Phones: (H) _____ (W) _____

Name: _____

Phones: (H) _____ (W) _____

INTERCESSORY PRAYER LIST

Cell Group Member:

Stress Areas:

Date	Prayer Need	By Faith, I See This Person:
___/___/___ ASKED ___/___/___ ANSWERED		
___/___/___ ASKED ___/___/___ ANSWERED		
___/___/___ ASKED ___/___/___ ANSWERED		
___/___/___ ASKED ___/___/___ ANSWERED		
___/___/___ ASKED ___/___/___ ANSWERED		

Reaching Out to Unbelievers

Tony, Sandy, Dean,
Dave, Penny
next mtg. Sat Morning

Tuesday @ Tony's for
make up
3 & 4 (1 & 2 are very basic)

> "A new command I give you: Love one another. As I have loved you, so you must love one another. By this all men will know that you are my disciples, if you love one another." — John 13:34-35

Reaching Out to Unbelievers

Pre-Christians

How many of you were reached for Christ through:

- ☑ Crusade evangelism *BGEA + JBIP*
- ☐ Door-to-door visitation
- ☐ Street evangelism
- ☐ Pastoral visitation
- ☐ A television program
- ☐ Visiting a church
- ☑ Personal relationship *90% of todays ch. members*

Brother, Maureen are led to Christ this way

Of those who checked something other than "Personal relationship," how many were influenced by a friend or family member to consider Christ?

If personal relationships are so effective in reaching people, why do you think the church spends so much energy on other means of evangelism?

intensity
strong preaching

Spontaneous Evangelism

> "My prayer is not for them alone. I pray also for those who will
> believe in me through their message, that all of them may be one,
> Father, just as you are in Me and I am in You. May they also be in Us
> so that the world may believe that You have sent Me .... May they
> be brought to complete unity to let the world know that you sent Me
> and have loved them even as You have loved Me."
> — John 17:20-23

Reach flows out of

• True spiritual unity in the body leads to evangelism.

flows

- Don't fall into the trap of believing that groups are made
   for fellowship alone.

- True fellowship will lead to the desire to share and express
   the joy of the fellowship.

• Small group evangelism should spontaneously flow out of the
   life shared in Christ.

  • *personal testimonies*
    All group members need to
    be able to share theirs
    in 3 minutes or less

  - *most Christians do not*
    have or nurture
    relationships = pre-Christians

LARGE GROUP ACTIVITY

> *"Every small group or church needs to have some form of evangelism going on in order to maintain health."*[1] — Steve Sjogren

How do you respond to the above quote?

Love the Lord ī all my heart, soul, mind & strength - & neighbor as myself WORD -

Make a list of the roadblocks to spontaneous evangelism in the church. *- lack of genuine love for God, others & self.*

Step 1: Focus the Group on the Vision

• Clarify the vision of the group.

  - Do not wait until the group is established to cast the vision of reaching/people. *out* *To pre-Christians*

• Help people wrestle with the call to ~~evangelism~~. *outreach to outsiders*

   - Many people have a great fear of evangelism.

   - Most people don't understand how to reach out to others.

ROADBLOCKS: TIME, LACK of intensionality, misunderstanding appropriate roles & responsibilities

• Spend time during each meeting focusing Outward during the Witness portion of the meeting. Ideas include:

   - Sharing the group's vision to reach ~~the lost~~. *outsiders*

   - Identifying friends who ~~don't~~ *MAY NOT* know Jesus.

   - Praying for ~~the lost~~. *pre-Christians*

   - Planning a party or other activity to which you can invite outsiders.

   - Discussing how you are ministering to your ~~unbelieving~~ *preChristian* friends.

Praying for that empty chair - Group prayer for an individual someone is developing an outreach relationship -

> "Any enterprise begins to die when it's run for the benefit of the insider rather than for the benefit of outsiders."[2] — Peter Drucker

Step 2: Make Your Group Visitor-Friendly

• Meet Consistently –

  - Once per week.

  - Same night and time.

  - If you rotate homes, make sure you communicate <u>well</u> with potential newcomers.

• Stay Small

  - When a group grows to 12 or more, newcomers feel left out.

• Reject the "family-reunion" mentality.

  - Inside jokes and common group stories are fun for the old members, but they exclude newcomers.

  - Avoid "religious" jargon. Words like "justification," "redemption," and "transcendence" will communicate to new people that they are not invited to participate.

• Make newcomers feel welcome.

  - Spend a little <u>extra</u> time on <u>an icebreaker</u> so that everyone can get to know one another.

Q: milk vs meat "in depth" of Bible Study - Carefully select Study Topics - "How does the Bible relate to this subject"

• Follow up on newcomers.

    - Get their phone numbers and/or addresses.

spouse & kid's names

    - Call them or send a card the next day. —

Step 3: Make Contact with ~~the Lost~~ *outsiders*

• Servant Evangelism

    - Hold a totally free car wash.

    - Give away soft drinks.

    - Rake leaves for others as an act of kindness.

    - Tell them, that you are doing this as a practical way to share God's love with them.
READ —

    - See *101 Ways to Reach Your Community* by Steve Sjogren.[3]

• Focus on your neighborhood. —

    - Spend time in your front yard.

    - Go for walks and talk with people who are outside.

    - Prayer walk your neighborhood.

    - Hold a block party.

- open house during holidays
- make goodies
- help new neighbors i practical things

Do this!

PERSONAL ACTIVITY

Take some time to list those people in your life who do not know Jesus below:

YOUR FRIENDSHIP PRAYER LIST

Who are the people in your circle of influence that don't know Jesus as Lord and Savior? Write their names in the spaces provided:

1. _____   5. _____

2. _____   6. _____

3. _____   7. _____

4. _____   8. _____

Now, circle the names of one or two unbelievers who are open to the *message* of Jesus Christ in addition to you, the *messenger*. They would probably come to a Bible study or visit your cell meeting if you pray for them daily and ask them repeatedly. These people are searching for something, and they may not know what they are looking for. You should focus more time and effort on these people, because they are ripe for harvest.

SMALL GROUP ACTIVITY

In groups of 3 or 4, spend time praying for the people you circled.

Step 4: Develop Relationships with ~~the Lost~~ *outsiders*

- Deepen the level of conversation as trust increases.

  - Review the levels of conversation in Session 4.

- Ask people how you can pray for them.

  - Few people reject prayer.

  - Sometimes you will be able to pray for them (on the spot.)

> *"Evangelism will be effective . . . in direct proportion to its dependence on the establishment and cultivation of meaningful relationships."*
> — Wayne McDill

- Invite people to the "fun things" your group does.

  Pot lucks, bowling, game nights, scavenger hunts, throw a "Matthew" party.

- Start a children's cell group in your neighborhood.

  - Many adults are reached through their children.

  - Start visiting the children in their homes.

- Watch for "stress events" that open doors for ministry. These include:

  - Death of family member

Outnumber the ~~people~~ Christians = the outsiders.

Grander Vision starts on my knees praying first thing & asking God for a way to show love to people around me

- Change in job situation

"The highest high & lowest low experienced this week."

- Trouble with son or daughter

- Loss of a close friend

"radical inclusion"

- Serious illness *we don't need to fix or straighten 'em out*
- New baby born
- Neighborhood yard sales

Step 5: Plant Seeds of the Gospel

• Invite people to a special harvest event.

  - Concert or special event.

  - Easter or Christmas worship celebration.

• If open, invite them to your cell group or weekly celebration.

• Start an Exploratory Bible Study.

  - 6-8 weeks in length.

  - Use something like *Introducing Jesus* by Pete Scazzaro.[4]

• Share the *Jesus Video*.[5]

"I could not pray for you"

Step 6: Be Prepared to Harvest

- Look for opportunities to ask something like this:

    - "What did you think about what you heard the pastor say the other night?"

    - "What did you think about the *Jesus* film we watched last night?"

- Engage the seeker in meaningful conversation that flows out of his answer if appropriate.

- Be prepared to use the Scriptures to show how one becomes a Christian.

- 2. "What is the greatest issue facing the country, world, your family today?

- 1. "What is the basis you use to solve problems in your life?

3.

A Simple 5-Part Process for Relationship Evangelism[6]

1. Target one or two.

   - Everyone in the group chooses one or two of their friends, coworkers, family members, or neighbors who do not know Jesus.

2. Pray

   - It's very difficult to minister to someone when you have not heard from the Lord how to minister to them.

   - It is even more difficult to love someone, when the love of God does not flow out of your heart for that person.

3. Pray together.

   - Form a list of those that the cell group members are praying for.

   - Use something like the _Blessing List_ to facilitate this process.

4. Work on the relationship.

   Establishing Friendships –
   + Cultivating Friendships –
   + Relational Evangelism –
   = Spontaneous Growth

5. Do fun things.

   - As a group, plan fun activities to which you can invite non-Christians.
   pre-

Recommended Reading

How To Lead a Great Cell Group Meeting by Joel Comiskey, Chapter 8.

101 Ways to Reach Your Community by Steve Sjogren.

*Walking Together
through
the Stages of Group Life*

"My command is this: Love each other as I have loved you. Greater love has no one than this, that he lay down his life for his friends. You are my friends if you do what I command. I no longer call you servants, because a servant does not know his master's business. Instead, I have called you friends, for everything that I learned from my Father I have made known to you." — John 15:12-15

Walking Together through the Stages of Group Life

The Development of Authentic Relationships

- Friendships develop through a process that begins with superficial interaction and progresses to deep acceptance and love.

- Group relationships develop in a similar pattern.

  - They form on a superficial level.

  - They storm by working through differences.

  - They norm by accepting and loving one another.

  - They perform by working together as a team.

  - They reform by following God into new group ministry.

- The graph on the next page illustrates the bonding process.

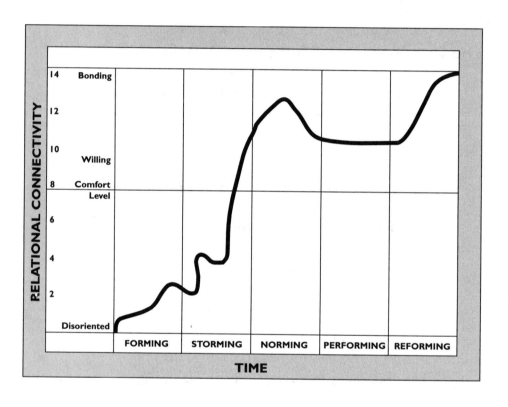

*several recommended food &
good leadership during this
time*

Forming Stage — What Can You Expect?

- Participation

    - "Maybe I can find true friends."

    - "Maybe this is a place where I can grow and serve."

    - "Maybe this group will be fun and exciting."

- Anxiety

    - "Do I feel included in this group?"

    - "Do I want to include others in my life?"

- Superficial Relationships

    - "I hope they don't discover how I act outside of church."

    - "I cannot share what I really think; they might reject me."

    - "Jim's comment hurt me, but maybe it will get better."

- Tenuous Environment

    - "Is this the kind of group I want to be a part of?"

    - "What qualifies Sharon for group leadership?"

    - "If I don't come back, can I still be a part of this church?"

• Some call this stage pseudo-community.

- Group members look like they are getting along on the surface.

- Yet people do not know one another well enough to truly accept and love one another.

Leadership Initiatives during the Forming Stage:

• Take charge as the leader.

- Group members are waiting for the leader to lead.

- Statements like: "What do you want from this group? I'll lead you where you want to go," communicate that the group has no purpose.

- Communicate your vision and what you have heard God say about the group.

- One group meets Monday night so they can use Awana as their sitter for the kids.

- Be time conscious - day of the wk. is critical.

- Soup gathering - teens can join in - adults.

- Fun activity vs kicking the group off too fast or too stringent a schedule

*Confidentiality clearly
Communicated.
- No gossip or
ratting on teates, etc.*

SESSION 7

- Communicate <u>the purpose</u> of the group's existence.

  - Community

  - Personal Growth / Life Transformation

  - Body Life

  - Lifestyle / Friendship Evangelism

  - Pastoral Care

  - Group Multiplication

- Develop a group covenant. —

  - This helps the group understand the boundaries of the group so that they know what group participation means.

  - See the sample covenant at the end of this session.

- Target new people.

  - It is natural to add new people to a newly forming group.

  - Find people in your church who are not already members of a group.

  - Invite friends from outside the church to check out your new group.

• Facilitate safe interaction.

- Focus on communication levels 1-3. (See pages 45-46)

- Use the first meeting to get acquainted by using multiple icebreakers.

THIS SET OF FOUR QUESTIONS WORKS WELL:

1. Where did you live between the ages of 7 and 12 and how many brothers and sisters did you have?

2. What kind of car did your family have?

3. Who was the person closest to you?

4. When did God become more than a word to you?

- In the next three meetings, use history-giving icebreakers.

- Ask some people to share their testimonies briefly.

Storming Stage — What Can You Expect?

• Disappointment

- With one another.

- With the group's progress toward achieving its goals and objectives.

• Conflict

- Due to past hurts that are brought to the group.

- Due to misunderstanding.

- Due to hurtful statements left unaddressed.

• Apathy

- Toward the group's goals and objectives.

- Toward attending group meetings.

- Toward personal spiritual growth.

• Questioning of Leadership

- Doubt about the leadership ability of the cell group leader.

- Potential to misunderstand church leaders.

• Spiritual Warfare

- There is amazing power in couples praying together, the enemy is trying to prevent that.

- Satan takes advantage of the members' self-centeredness.

Don't be afraid to get help if conflicts become hurtful or divisive.

CHG Leaders, Pastors

LARGE GROUP ACTIVITY

Make a list of reasons why many small groups never move through the Storming Stage even though they continue meeting.

- afraid to disagree or have conflict
- adding new folks
- brushing conflict under the rug.

Pressing through the Storming Stage

• The only way to weather the storm is to empty yourself.

> *Let the same mind be in you that was in Christ Jesus, who, though He was in the form of God, did not regard equality with God as something to be exploited, but <u>emptied</u> Himself, taking the form of a slave, being born in human likeness.* — Philippians 2:5-7 NRSV

- Prejudices.

- Preconceived ideas about what would happen in the group.

- The desire to control others and even your own emotions.

- Individual ambitions, desires, and goals that stand in the way of the group's goals.

- The expectation that others will act and think like you do.

- The hope that everyone in the group will be as spiritually mature as you are.

- When group members <u>empty themselves</u>, humility has room to move in. *Leaders go first!*

  - Members can work past the surface irritants of others.

  - Members recognize that they also have surface irritants that others dislike.

  - Members discover the power of listening to understand, instead of hearing to judge.

Leadership Initiatives during the Storming Stage:

- Don't be surprised by the storm.

  - Watch the group's interaction and learn to recognize it.

  - Help the group understand that tension and even chaos are normal parts of developing authentic relationships.

- Don't try to control the storm.

  - Many fail to <u>listen to the concerns</u> and hurts of those in the group.

  - Others try to organize the storm so that people can hide from the conflict. This can be done by overemphasizing safe Bible study questions or by strategically keeping people apart when there are issues that need dealing with.

  - Instead, pray and discuss.

• Meet the stage with confidence.

   - Meet privately with those in conflict.

   - Stay calm. A calm leader brings calmness to the group.

   - Speak the truth in love as the Spirit leads.

• Help people understand one another's differences.

   - Different personalities.

   - Different beliefs.

   - Different backgrounds.

   - Different interests.

• Enlist help from church leaders.

• Focus the group on an outside ministry task.

> "Lasting relationships are not negotiated. . . . They are forged. That means heat and pressure. It is commitment to a relationship which sustains it . . . not pleasant feelings. Treat a relationship as negotiable — it is easily lost. Consider it nonnegotiable — a way is found to make it work."[1] — Richard C. Halverson

SMALL GROUP ACTIVITY

Identify the type of person below who tends to get on your nerves the quickest. Why?

Pick one person from your past with one of these characteristics. How did you deal with your relationship with that person?

Norming Stage — What Can You Expect?

- Harmony, respect, intimacy, and trust.

    - Members spontaneously spend time with one another.

    - When personal problems occur, people naturally reach out to another cell group member.

- Loving accountability.

    - Members openly confess struggles.

    - They desire help, feedback, and accountability.

- Group identity has developed.

- Potential Dangers:

    - "Group think," where group members begin to think alike and stop challenging one another.

    - "Nesting" keeps the group in a comfortable situation and limits the future potential to reach other people and add them to the group.

- Identify the apprentice right up front so that purpose is accepted from the beginning

- rebirthing process not a break-up, but more of a necessity

- Keep the "empty chair" visible

Leadership Initiatives during the Norming Stage:

- Reinforce the vision and the purpose of the group.

  - Invite the pastor or another corporate church leader to visit and share the church's vision.

  multiplication

  - Spend extended times of prayer together focusing on God's purposes. *"Now as you are going, make disciples..."*

- Minister to and with one another.

  - Allow more time for personal ministry in your group meetings.

  - Utilize the *Blessing List* to bring a concerted emphasis on praying for lost friends and acquaintances.[2]

  - Use group-sponsored events to cultivate relationships with lost friends.

  - Create opportunities for members to serve together two-by-two and three-by-three.

- Equip members for ministry.

  - Delegate leadership responsibilities.
  icebreaker, worship, snacks, prayer, journaling
  - Encourage members to progress through the church's equipping materials.

Performing Stage — What Can You Expect?

- Teamwork

- Group ownership

- Ministry competence

    - Pastoral care within the group

    - Compassionate ministry outside the group

    - Prayer

- New group members

- Accelerated development

    - This stage does not last very long.

    - When people are added to the group, you must have a plan how the group will move Forward.

"Forming spiritual community is the Spirit's work. Most of what we do is give up control, get out of the way, and let the Spirit take over. More than anything else, we pray."[3] — Larry Crabb

Leadership Initiatives during the Performing Stage:

• Challenge

  - Recognize risk takers.

  - Encourage people to step out and minister.

  - Show people how to minister to those outside the group.

• Organize

  - Plan group harvest events focused on reaching lost persons.

  - Invite lost friends to church-sponsored harvest events, area Christian concerts, and other events.

• Delegate

  - At this point, the official cell leader should be leading the meeting less and less as he delegates the parts of the meeting to potential leaders.

  - Pray about the group's future multiplication.

SMALL GROUP ACTIVITY

Place an "X" on the line below that marks the stage of your current group.

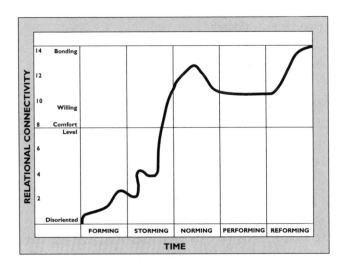

How long do you think your group has been in this stage?

What can you do to help advance your current group to the next stage?

Recommended Reading

• *How to Lead a Great Cell Group Meeting* by Joel Comiskey, Chapter 9.

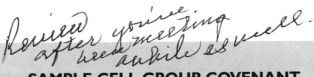

Review you're after week meeting auhile as well.

SAMPLE CELL GROUP COVENANT

Because God has called me to love and be loved, I covenant to:

Participate. I commit to be a part of this group and choose to be present regularly at the cell group meetings.

Affirm. I will accept others in love and work through any preconceived notions or expectations I have of them so that we can become friends.

Make Myself Available. If someone in this group needs my time, support, energy, or insight, I will be there to help them.

Be On Time. Recognizing tardiness often demonstrates a disrespect for others, I will do my best to arrive at group meetings on time.

Honestly Share. I choose to grow in my ability to share myself with the people in my group so they will discover who I am: my joys, my struggles, my hopes, and my disappointments.

Pray. I pledge to pray regularly for my group, my group leader, and myself as I contribute to the group.

Listen. I promise to suspend my judgment of others in the group and truly seek to understand who they are. I want to learn about who they are: their gifts and their needs, their strengths and their joys, their weaknesses and their struggles.

Keep Confidentiality. I will keep in confidence what is shared within the confines of the group, whether shared in a group meeting, in a one-on-one discussion, or in social interaction.

Serve Non-Christians. I commit to both showing and sharing the love of Jesus with people outside this group in hopes that those who do not know Jesus will soon receive His love and forgiveness through the ministry of this group.

Discover My Calling. I will seek God for His destiny, knowing that He has gifted me for ministry. I will be open to the guidance of the leadership in my cell and in my church about the possibility of my one day leading a group.

In turn, because this group is committed to bless the members of the group, the leadership covenants to:

Start and End the Meeting On Time. The cell group meeting is not a time to deal with every ministry need. If you want to remain after the meeting, feel free to do so, but you don't need to feel guilty if you need to leave.

Meet Weekly. True relationships are built upon regular interaction. This group is committed to weekly interaction so that we can become a supportive network for one another.

Minister to Your Needs. In this group, we will listen to you and pray that God will reveal how to minister to you as He knows best. We will submit to His leadership and follow Him as he leads us to minister to you.

Seek Help from Leaders When Needed. The leadership of the church, its resources, and many other training tools are available to minister to you. The leadership of this group will seek additional input about how best to minister to you.

Help You Minister through Spiritual Gifts. In this group, you will be encouraged and depended upon to hear from God and receive power from Him to minister to others.

Lead You to Discover Your Passion and Calling to Minister. Every member has the potential to minister effectively and lead others. You are no exception.

Reach Out to Non-Christians. This group will not become self-focused. It will seek ways to lovingly include your friends and family so that they too might experience Christ's love.

Birth a New Group. This group will make plans to start a new group as one of the cell group members is raised up and prepared to become a leader.

Reforming Groups by Producing Leaders

You then, my son, be strong in the grace that is in Christ Jesus. And the things you have heard me say in the presence of many witnesses entrust to reliable men who will also be qualified to teach others.
— 2 Timothy 2:1-2

Reforming Groups by Producing Leaders

Reform or Deform

- Every group has a choice. (See graph on next page)

  - It can reform by starting new groups.

  - It can deform and become ineffective.

- Acts 2:46-47 reveals that God's intention is for the church to multiply and to reproduce.

Every day they continued to meet together in the temple courts. They broke bread in their homes and ate together with glad and sincere hearts, praising God and enjoying the favor of all the people. And the Lord added to their number daily those who were being saved.
— Acts 2:46-47

- Reproduction is a natural part of life.

  Groups that are full of life will reproduce.

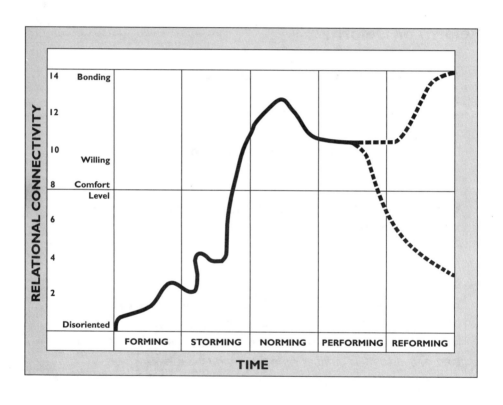

LARGE GROUP ACTIVITY

Make a short list of reasons why people resist reproduction and multiplication: *Comfort   Group resistence to change.*
lack of maturity
Logistics - childcare, transfers & moves
losing touch = members of the group

Five Steps to Reforming a Group

Prepare	Recruit	Equip	Release	Reform
→	→	→	→	→
Pray, watch, and try out	Discern and select a potential leader -	Train and mentor potential leader	Release new leader to do more and more ministry in the group	Support new leader as she/*he* starts a new group

Shifting to →

CLG Leader →   →

Act as Primary Leader | **Act as Coach and Trainer**

Facilitates
- ~~Lead~~ all group meetings
- *delegates responsibilites*
- Minster to most needs outside the meeting

- Share leading of all meetings
- Share all ministry outside the meeting

Adapted with permission from Gareth Icenogle

1 Peter 2:9 — Each believer is a royal "priest" in God's kingdom w/ heavenly potential

Step I — Prepare Every Member for Ministry

• See every group member as a
potential leader.

ministry facilitator

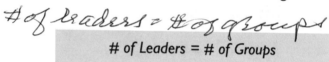

L = Leader
PL = Potential
    Leader

(• Focus on developing people.)

  - A new group is the result of the launching of a new leader.

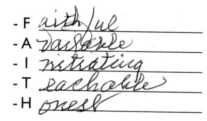

# of Leaders = # of Groups

  - Develop people through relational investment.

• Try before you buy.

  - Many people recruit apprentices or interns first before
    testing them.

    - F *aithful*
    - A *vailable*
    - I *nitiating*
    - T *eachable*
    - H *onest*

• Delegate simple ministry tasks.

    Potential Facilitator

1. Invite the ~~rising leader~~ to accompany you as you minister,
   explaining what you are doing.

2. Ask her to observe and to participate in some way.

110

3. Debrief afterward, asking what was observed, and how it could be done differently.

Facilitate

- Possible ministry opportunities:
  - Lead the icebreaker *segment*
  - Organize the worship for the cell meeting
  - Call a newcomer *follow up č a visitor*
  - Organize a cell group <u>social gathering</u>
  - Go with you to visit someone in the hospital
  - Visit a family for a prayer visit
  - Enlist, <u>for a period of three months</u>, an
    Upward Captain
    Inward Captain
    Outward Captain — *help organize service projects*

Ministry opportunities: outreach service.

COMMUNICATING THE VISION FOR CELL REPRODUCTION

1. Be convinced that cell growth, development of apprentice leaders, and multiplication are part of God's plan for the health and the future of the church.

2. Introduce the reproduction process <u>early</u> and <u>often</u>. <u>Talk</u> <u>about your plan to multiply at the outset of your group</u>.

3. Recognize that the availability and readiness of the intern/ apprentice is the key. No time schedule or even the rapid growth of a cell should dictate when a cell should multiply. The readiness of a new leader is the true indicator that a cell is ready and able to successfully reproduce.

Step 2 — ~~Recruit~~ Those Who Prove Ready

Invite, Present an opportunity to

- Identify the potential leader or leaders who are the most ready to lead a future group.

- Only ~~recruit~~ *invite* people for a position like an intern/apprentice <u>after</u> they are already performing part of the responsibilities of that position.

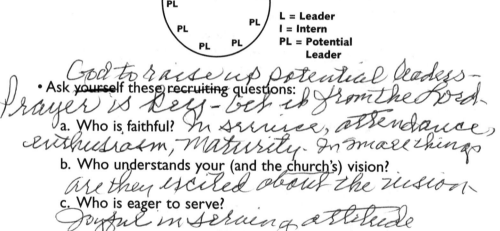

L = Leader
I = Intern
PL = Potential Leader

- Ask ~~yourself~~ these recruiting questions:

God to raise up potential leaders — Prayer is key — bet it from the Lord.

  a. Who is faithful? *In service, attendance, enthusiasm, maturity. In small things*

  b. Who understands your (and the church's) vision? *Are they excited about the vision*

  c. Who is eager to serve? *Joyful in serving attitude*

  d. Who is God pointing out? *Prayer is key —*

  e. Who seems to lead the group even without a position?

  f. Who has the ability to train others? *Thought leaders — Tim, Patience, Clear communicator, example of Christ in character*

- Discuss with your pastor or cell coach <u>before</u> recruiting. *affirm that God has truly called this person*

JESUS DIDN'T CHOOSE
THE STAR PLAYERS

and how He selected them-

Jesus is our model. We would be wise to look at whom He chose. He gathered people around Himself who were not looking for leadership, and did not have a large agenda to play out (except Judas).

He chose an array of common people, ignorant people, and people who were despised by their fellow men. Why would He do this? Why didn't He look for people who were highly gifted and skilled? Those who were schooled in communication skills, theology, doctrine, and interpersonal relations? Because He did only what His Father was telling Him to do (John 14:6-11), and His Father had a long track record of choosing the common person (Moses- Exodus 3:4-12; Isaiah-Isaiah 6:1-9; David-1 Samuel 16:1-13). The kind of people you and I would probably write off as less than worthy of leadership.

> *"All a man's ways seem right to him, but the LORD weighs the heart."* — Proverbs 21:2

Yet in three short years He turned the church, under the inspiration and guidance of the Holy Spirit, over to this rag-tag group of people. Even people who abandoned Him in His greatest moment of sorrow and need were entrusted with this huge task.

—Thom Corrigan

Step 3 — Equip Your Intern(s)/Apprentice(s)

• Jesus modeled how to delegate:

1. Your intern watches you.

2. You explain what you did and why you did it.

3. You observe as the intern does the same thing.

4. You objectively identify strengths and weaknesses you observed.

5. You provide training to strengthen the weaknesses.

6. You turn the task over to your intern.

7. You withdraw, using "benign neglect" as your strategy.

8. You continue to monitor and encourage your intern.

• Practical ways to equip your intern/apprentice:

- Take your intern with you on every ministry opportunity.

- Let him lead the cell group meeting.

- Let her keep in touch with 1/2 of the cell group members.

- Encourage him to take the cell group leader training at your church.

- Meet with her every week to discuss personal discipleship issues, cell ministry, and relationship development.

PERSONAL ACTIVITY

To help you gauge your effectiveness at releasing others into ministry, answer the following questions

YES / NO

_✓_ ____ 1. Do you develop close friendships with those you are leading?

_✓_ ____ 2. Do you enlist others to help you even though they might make a mistake?

____ _✓_ 3. When releasing tasks to an apprentice, do you allow him to take on responsibility a little at a time until full competence is achieved?

____ _✓_ 4. When others are responsible for carrying on without you, does it run smoothly and are tasks completed to your satisfaction?
not always

____ _✓_ 5. When you have assigned a task to someone, do you spend time with her afterwards to discuss how it went?
not as often as I should.

____ _✓_ 6. Do you get more joy from doing a task yourself than from seeing trainee doing the task successfully?

____ ____ 7. In training another, do you put the trainee in the hot seat quickly, which sometimes leads to embarrassing mistakes?
I have in the past but am learning otherwise

_✓_ ____ 8. When charged with accomplishing a task, are you prone to do it yourself so that it is done the way you want?

____ _✓_ 9. When someone you have trained makes a poor decision, are you more likely to overrule that decision yourself than to work with the person directly to reevaluate the decision?

_____ ✓ _____ 10. When someone performs less than satisfactorily, do you ignore the poor performance to avoid hurting feelings?

Scoring the Assessment

For questions 1-5:   Give yourself one point for each "Yes" answer: 3___
For questions 6-10: Give yourself one point for each "No" answer: ___
Total Points: ___

If you score between:

1-5 points: Seek training and guidance from a mentor before assuming a role where you are responsible for mentoring and overseeing others.

6-8 points: Go forward in leading and mentoring others, but realize you have some weaknesses that may hurt your efforts. Seek guidance and oversight from more experienced mentors.

9-10 points: Mentor others with confidence. Help others mentor in similar ways as you do.

Step 4 — Release the Ministry of the Group to Those You Have Equipped

• Encourage Profusely

   - Practice the 8:2 Principle

• Give away your ministry.

   - At first you are doing 80% of the ministry.

   - At the end of the group you should only be doing about 20% of the ministry.

```
┌─────────────────────────────────────────┐
│                                           │
│   Your Ministry                           │
│                                           │
│                                           │
│                Your Intern's Ministry     │
│                                           │
└─────────────────────────────────────────┘
```

LARGE GROUP ACTIVITY

List reasons why encouragement is so vital to leadership development: *it creates confidence. its Scriptural, creates enthusiasm + hope. lets people know you really care*

> "A leader is one who, because of good character qualities, is able to influence others in a positive way."[1] — Jeff Arnold

Step 5 — *Forming of* Birthing a New Group

• When a group processes through the first four steps, birthing is a very natural result.

- When a new leader is ready to start a group, release him or her to do so.

   - You do not need to wait until a group has gone through all of the stages discussed in Session 7.

- Warning: Do not birth because your group is too big.

   - Birth a new group <u>because someone is prepared and has a vision to lead a new group.</u>

   - When you birth out of necessity, it causes a great deal of trauma since people perceive it as a negative experience.

VISION QUESTIONS FOR BIRTHING NEW GROUPS

Write out a short statement that reflects the vision God has laid on your heart for a new group.

- Who do you envision participating (maybe a certain age group, or an un-grouped segment of your church or community)?

- Where will your group's ministry focus? Is there a certain neighborhood you want to reach?

- When will your group meet? Is there a specific time slot that people want?

- What do you want this group to accomplish?

Connect & grow

• Proven Strategies for Reforming Groups

1. New Leader Launch:
   New leader takes 2 to 3
   people to start a new
   group.

   Plant model

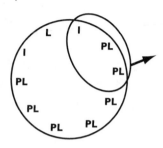

2. New Leader Plant:
   New leader plants a new
   group with new people.

   Pilot Groups this we'll do this

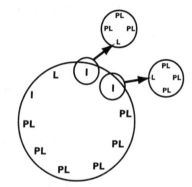

3. Old Leader Launch:
   New leader takes old group
   and old leader starts
   new group.

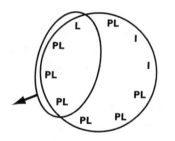

4. Organic Multiplication:
   New leader and old leader
   each lead groups by
   multiplying the old group.

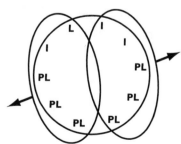

L = Leader, I = Intern, PL = Potential Leader

A SEVEN-STEP PROCESS FOR
ORGANIC MULTIPLICATION

1. Two months before multiplication, both cell group leaders should make a list of those people whom God has laid on their heart that should go with them to accomplish the vision God has given them.

2. The cell group leaders should meet and pray with their pastor or coach to determine how to multiply the group.

3. One month before multiplication, each of the projected groups should meet in two rooms for the Word portion of the meeting.

4. Each cell group leader should meet individually with all of those on his or her list and ask them to participate in the vision of his or her cell group.

5. Begin to gradually lead more and more of the meeting in two rooms of the same house until the group is only fellowshipping together before and after the meeting.

6. Multiply the group so that it is meeting at two different places.

7. Schedule a party for one month after the multiplication date.

Appendix

A

What Do We Do with the Children?

Appendix A

What Do We Do with the Children?

SMALL GROUP ACTIVITY

• Jesus and children

  - In groups of three, read and discuss the passage below:

> *People were bringing little children to Jesus to have him touch them, but the disciples rebuked them. When Jesus saw this, he was indignant. He said to them, "Let the little children come to me, and do not hinder them, for the kingdom of God belongs to such as these. I tell you the truth, anyone who will not receive the kingdom of God like a little child will never enter it." And he took the children in his arms, put his hands on them and blessed them. — Mark 10:13-6*

  - What stands out to you in this passage?

  - What words characterize the disciples' attitude toward children? What words characterize Jesus' attitude?

  - How did Jesus specifically love and minister to the children, according to these verses?

PERSONAL ACTIVITY

- Compare your attitudes to those of Jesus.

    - On the continuum below, place an 'X' to indicate where your attitude stands in relationship to that of Jesus and the disciples.

Disciples
Children:
Nuisance, Unimportant

Jesus
Children:
Valuable, Important

    - Based on the words of Jesus below, how well is your cell group currently doing in welcoming Christ? Indicate it by placing a 'C' on the continuum below.

> *"Whoever welcomes one of these little children in my name welcomes me; and whoever welcomes me does not welcome me but the one who sent me."* — Mark 9:37

Rejecting   **Tolerating**   **Welcoming**

    - What specifically would you like to see change in how your cell group relates to children?

Options for Ministering to the Children

- Intergenerational group with the children separating out to a Kids' Slot.

- Intergenerational group with the children participating completely in the meeting with the adults.

- Appoint a permanent Kids' Slot leader from outside the cell group.

- Children's cell group.

    - These are independent groups which have their own leaders.

The Intergenerational Cell Group

- What is an intergenerational cell group?

"An Intergenerational Cell Group is a cell group that welcomes children as full members. It does not set up any age barriers. Although the children may have a separate subgroup during the evening, they belong to the whole cell group and they can bless and minister to the adults as well as being blessed by the adults. Such cell groups include the children in all their activities: prayer, praise, spiritual growth and evangelism. Families and singles mix together to form a wider family of Christ."[1] — Lorna Jenkins

- It is a place where children and adults, married and single can find belonging.

- A caring fellowship, serving one another and reaching out to others.

- A group where adults are willing to relinquish some peace and quiet, late nights, and adult superiority.

• Advantages of intergenerational cell groups:

- For adults and children:
    Participation in one another's lives
    Family unity and growth
    A caring extended family of aunts, uncles, nieces,
        nephews, and cousins

- For children:
    Close observation of their parents' spiritual life and
    fellowship
    An expanded base of Christian role models
    The opportunity to learn how to pray, confess, and minister
    Christian community to bring friends

Establish Cell Group House Rules[2]

• The adults should address these questions:

- How will we involve the children?

- In what ways will we do our part in caring for and taking an interest in our children?

- In what areas do we need to be particularly aware that we are role models?

- How can we make the cell group a priority?

- How can we make the cell group a safe and trustworthy place for everyone?

- In what ways do we need to respect each other's homes?

- How will we address the issue of discipline with the children?

- What are our expectations of each other in the cell meeting?

- Is there anything we would particularly like to ask of the children?

- The children should consider these questions:

    - In what ways will we be careful to be kind and helpful?

    - How can we contribute to the meetings?

    - How can we be an encouragement to the other people in the group?

    - In what ways do we need to respect our parents and the other adults in the group?

    - How should we behave toward each other?

    - When we go to other people's homes, what do we need to be careful of?

    - What would we like to ask of the adults?

The Intergenerational Cell Group Meeting

- Welcome

    - Use an icebreaker question that even the children can answer, or offer them an alternative question.

    - Children (as adults) can always "pass" on the icebreaker.

    - Do not allow children to be rudely disruptive.
      (Age-appropriate disruptiveness should be expected and tolerated.)

- Brief Intergenerational Worship

    - Depending on the ages of the children include them for all or part of the worship time.

    - This can include one or two worshipful children's songs such as "Jesus Loves Me" and "Cast Your Burdens on Jesus."

- Word

    - Adults and children normally meet separately for the remaining part of the meeting until the fellowship time.

    - A Kids' Slot leader will lead the children.

- Witness

- Fellowship

    - Adults and children all share in the fellowship following the meeting.

    - It is important to end the meeting on time to allow time for relationship building that happens over fellowship and refreshments. Parents will be especially concerned that the evening does not go late.

- Periodic Options

  - Children are included for the entire meeting depending on the age and number of children.

  - Change the order of the meeting and how children are included and involved.

- Body Life

  - Include children in fun times, meals, work projects, and parties.

  - Involve children in outreach events and prayer walks.

  - Include adult-only times in the cell schedule as well.

The Kids' Slot

- What is a Kids' Slot?

"A small group of children bonded together around a leader for mutual care, prayer, questioning, and discussion. Living their Christian life together, they reach out to serve others and win other children to Jesus." — Lorna Jenkins

  - It is *not* baby sitting, a Bible study, or busy work.

  - It is a time for children to share together under adult direction in order to experience and encounter God.

• The Structure of the Kids' Slot

  - The cell leader should recruit a Children's Coordinator.

  - Led by at least one adult per group of children.

  - All willing adults (including the cell group leader) take turns in a rotation schedule organized by the group's Children's Coordinator.

  - Usually there are 6-10 children. If there are more than that, divide them into two smaller groups.

• Age Considerations

  - Infants are kept with parents and are taken out if they are crying.

  - Toddlers and preschoolers should have a short Bible story and prayer time, but it will be mostly play time.

  - Elementary school age is the target age for Kids' Slot; they enjoy it, look forward to it and often want to bring friends.

  - Some teens will want to be involved in an intergenerational cell group in addition to, or instead of, being in a teen cell group.

    Normally they will be with the adults during the edification and ministry time, but some will want to be included in the rotation to help with the Kids' Slot. They make excellent role models for the younger children.

• Evangelism and Kids' Slot

- Seek to reach children through parents and parents through children.

- If a child attends with his parents, he may want to stay with them during the meeting the first week.

- If a child comes to the cell group without her parents, 'adopt' her into another family. Then invite her parents to group parties and other social events.

Suggested Kids' Slot Format

Key: Do not think ministry *to* children; think equipping children *to minister.*

• Icebreaker

- Sit on the floor in a circle.

- Use a short icebreaker to help settle the group down.

- The adult leader might share a personal story from his or her own childhood at this point.

• Word

- Share the Bible story.

- Facilitate discussion with questions and activities.

- Share a time of fun activity related to the theme. This could be a craft or drama or involve a game or illustration.

- Memorize a Bible verse and practice saying it.

• Respond

- Stop and pray after hearing each of the children's requests; they will forget them if you wait!

- Encourage the children to pray for and minister to one another, allowing the Holy Spirit to work through them.

• Report

- Each Kids' Slot should have a notebook. That way, week by week, the leaders can look at the notebook to see what happened last week and what the group prayed for.

- Have each Kids' Slot leader write down for the following week's leader what they did and prayed for.

- Rejoice with the children in answered prayers, allowing this to build faith for future requests.

• Regroup with the adults

  - Share a memory verse, sing a song, interview a Bible character, or perform a skit.

  - End the meeting.

Recommended Reading

Families Learning Together Volumes 1-4 by Karen Henley.

Heirs Together by Daphne Kirk.

Appendix

B

Ministry Practicums

Practicum 1

- Read Ezekiel 34:1-6 quoted on page 19. Meditate on it every day this week.

- Think about:

  - What is the calling of a shepherd?

  - How do you feel about this calling?

  - Spend time each day praying for the heart of a shepherd.

Practicum 2

- Lead the worship in your group this week.

- Prepare by meeting with your cell group leader to pray for the meeting and to choose the way to lead worship.

- Get feedback from your cell group leader; discuss how the worship time went.

  - What was one thing that went well?

  - What could you have done better?

Practicum 3

- Lead the icebreaker in your group this week. Make sure to share with your cell group leader the question you plan to use.

- Talk with your cell group leader about the lesson before the meeting. Secure a copy of the lesson for yourself.

- Observe how he or she leads the discussion. Later, talk about the flow of the meeting with the cell group leader.

- Discuss with your leader the answers to these questions:

  - What did you see God doing?

  - What did you learn?

  - How did God use you?

Practicum 4

- Meet with your cell group leader and discuss how to facilitate the Word portion of the meeting. Make sure to get a copy of the cell lesson from him.

- Lead the Word portion of the meeting.

- After the meeting, briefly meet with your cell group leader to talk about the flow of the meeting. Discuss:

  - What did you see God doing?

  - What did you do well in leading the discussion?

  - What do you need to improve upon?

Practicum 5

- Call three people in the group, and get to know them better. If there is an opportunity, take time to pray with them.

- Go with your cell group leader on a home prayer visit to bless someone in your group.

Practicum 6

• Lead the Witness portion of your group's meeting this week.

• To prepare, meet with your cell group leader and discuss the best way to facilitate this time together.

• After the cell meeting, talk with your cell group leader.

- What did you do well?

- What needs improvement?

Practicum 7

• Oversee the entire cell group meeting this week.

• Delegate different parts of the meeting to other members of the group, excluding the cell group leader.

• Lead the Word portion yourself.

• Discuss these questions with your cell group leader:

- What was the easiest part of the meeting?

- What was the hardest part?

Practicum 8

- Meet with your cell group leader and identify those in your group who are the most likely to become cell group leaders in the future. Spend time praying for them.

- Write the names of the people you identified below and discuss these questions:

    -Why did you choose them?

    -What ministry opportunities can you give them?

End Notes

Session 1
[1] Charles Colson, *Kingdoms in Conflict* (Grand Rapids: Zondervan, 1987), n.p.
[2] Lynn Anderson, *They Smell Like Sheep* (West Monroe, LA: Howard, 1997), 40.
[3] Dietrich Bonhoeffer, *Life Together* (New York: Harper Collins, 1954), 36-37.

Session 2
[1] Bill Beckham, *The Second Reformation* (Houston, TX: TOUCH® Publications, 1995) 142.
[2] Gerrit Gustufson, "Are You Developing New Leaders", *Cell Group Journal*, Spring 2000, 10.

Session 3
[1] Douglas Steeve quoted in Loughlan Sofield, Rosine Hammell and Carroll Juliano, *Building Community* (Notre Dame, IN: Ave Maria Press, 1998), 153.

Session 4
[1] Adapted from Roberta Hestenes, *Using the Bible in Groups* (Philadelphia: The Westminster Press, 1983), 96-97.

Session 5
[1] Carl George, *Nine Keys to Effective Small Group Leadership* (Mansfield, PA: Kingdom Publishing, 1997), 80.
[2] Ralph W. Neighbour, Jr., *The Shepherd's Guidebook* (Houston, TX: TOUCH® Publications, Revised Edition, 1996), 93.

End Notes

Session 6

[1] Steven Sjogren, *101 Ways to Reach Your Community* (Colorado Springs, CO: NavPress, 2001), 12.

[2] Peter Drucker quoted in Sofield, 103.

[3] Available through NavPress at 1-800-366-7788 or your local bookstore.

[4] Available through Intervarsity Press at 1-800-843-9487 or your local bookstore.

[5] For information on securing this video call 1-888-Jesus-36 or visit www.jesusvideo.org.

[6] Developed by Jay Firebaugh, used with permission.

Session 7

[1] Richard C. Halverson, *Somehow Inside of Eternity*, 63, quoted in Gorman, 217.

[2] The *Blessing List* is available through TOUCH® Publications at 1-800-735-5865 or visit www.cellgrouppeople.com.

[3] Larry Crabb, *The Safest Place on Earth* (Nashville: Word Publishing, 1999), 125.

Session 8

[1] Jeffrey Arnold, *The Big Book on Small Groups* (Dawners Grove, IL: Inter Varsity Press, 1992), 57.

Appendix A

[1] Lorna Jenkins, *Feed My Lambs* (Singapore: TOUCH Ministries International Pte Ltd, 1995), 22.

[2] Daphne Kirk, *What Shall We Do with the Children: An Equipping Manual for Cell Church Trainers* (Suffolk: Kevin Mayhew, 2000), 78-80. Used with permission.

ADDITIONAL CELL GROUP RESOURCES

HOW TO LEAD A GREAT CELL GROUP MEETING ...

... So People Want to Come Back *by Joel Comiskey*
Joel Comiskey takes you beyond theory and into the "practical tips of the trade" that will make your cell group gathering vibrant! This hands-on guide covers all you need to know, from basic how-to's of getting the conversation started to practical strategies for dynamic ministry times. If you're looking to find out what really makes a cell group meeting great . . . this book has the answers! 144 pgs.

8 HABITS OF EFFECTIVE SMALL GROUP LEADERS *by Dave Earley*
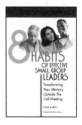
After years of leading and overseeing growing small groups, Pastor Dave Earley has identified 8 core habits of effective leaders. When adopted, these habits will transform your leadership too. The habits include: Dreaming • Prayer • Invitations • Contact Preparation • Mentoring • Fellowship • Growth.

When you adopt and practice these habits, your cell group will move from a once-a-week meeting to an exciting ministry to one another and the lost! 144 pgs.

LEADING FROM THE HEART *by Michael Mack*

Recharge your cell leadership! Powerful cell leaders share a common trait: a passionate heart for God. They know their priorities and know that time with Him is always at the top of the list.

If you have a sense that you are tired of ministry or frustrated with people, this title will help! If you have a great attitude and you want to go to the next level, this book will move you into new fields, white for harvest! 152 pgs.

UPWARD, INWARD, OUTWARD, FORWARD WORKBOOK
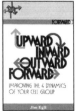
Improving the 4 Dynamics of Your Cell Group *by Jim Egli*
This easy to use workbook, combined with the facilitator's presentation will help your cell group grow in the four basic dynamics of healthy cell life. Upward: Deepening your relationship to the Father; Inward: Deepening community between cell members; Outward: Reaching the lost for Jesus successfully; Forward: Developing and releasing new leaders. 72-page student workbook.

Order Toll-Free from TOUCH® Outreach Ministries
1-800-735-5865 • Order Online: www.cellgrouppeople.com

ADDITIONAL CELL GROUP RESOURCES

THE JOURNEY GUIDE FOR CELL GROUP LEADERS

This tool will point you in the right direction as it helps you to understand the areas of leadership where you are strong and those areas that need improvement. You need not worry any longer about what you need to do as a leader. This tool will guide you. 16 pgs.

303 ICEBREAKERS: 303 ways to really "BREAK THE ICE"

You will never need another icebreaker book. This collection places at your fingertips easy-to-find ideas divided into nine categories, such as "Including the Children," "When a Visitor Arrives" and "Lighthearted and Fun." This is a needed reference for every cell meeting. We've included instructions on how to lead this part of the meeting effectively. 156 pgs.

OUR BLESSING LIST POSTER

Growing cell churches have proven that constant prayer for the lost yields incredible results! Use this nifty poster to list the names of your *oikos* and pray for them every time you meet. 34" x 22", folds down to 8.5" x 11" and comes with a handout master, equipping track and a master prayer list. Pack of 10.

Make Cell Groups Work Online!

Our website was designed for leaders just like you!

- Free articles from *CellChurch Magazine* & *CellGroup Journal.*

- Fast and secure online resource purchases.

- Watch a streaming video on the cell movement.

- Find other churches with cell groups in your area or denomination.

- Post your resume or search for a new staff member in our cell-based classifieds area.

- Free downloads of leader's guides, presentations, and software to track cell growth.

- Interact with other pastors and experts in our bulletin board forum.

What are you waiting for?

Grab a cup of coffee and visit us now...

www.cellgrouppeople.com